TRUTH SERUM PRESS ·

glow

truth serum vol. 6

First published as a collection September 2020
Content copyright © Truth Serum Press and individual authors
Edited by Matt Potter

BP#00095

Truth Serum Press
32 Meredith Street
Sefton Park SA 5083
Australia

Email: truthserumpress@live.com.au
Website: https://truthserumpress.net/
Store: https://truthserumpress.net/catalogue/

Original front cover image copyright © Lisa Runnels
Cover design copyright © Matt Potter

ISBN: 978-1-922427-12-0

Also available as an eBook
ISBN: 978-1-922427-13-7

A note on differences in punctuation and spelling:
Truth Serum Press proudly features writers from all over the English-speaking
world. Some speak and write English as their first language, while for others,
it's their second or third or even fourth language. Naturally, across all
versions of English, there are differences in punctuation and spelling, and
even in meaning. These differences are reflected in the work *Truth Serum
Press* publishes, and they account for any differences in punctuation, spelling
and meaning found within these pages.

Truth Serum Press is a member of the
Bequem Publishing collective
http://www.bequempublishing.com/

glow

(gloʊ)

1. countable noun [usually singular]

A glow is a dull, steady light, for example the light produced by a fire when there are no flames.

The rising sun casts a golden glow over the fields.

from **Collins Online English Dictionary**
https://www.collinsdictionary.com/dictionary/english/

glow

(gloʊ)

4. verb

If something glows, it produccs a dull, stcady light.

The night lantern glowed softly in the darkness.

from **Collins Online English Dictionary**
https://www.collinsdictionary.com/dictionary/english/

We are the Dead. Short days ago

We lived, felt dawn, saw sunset glow,

  Loved and were loved, and now we lie

    In Flanders fields.

from **In Flanders Fields**

by John McCrae

· Sara ABEND-SIMS · Ed AHERN · Tobi ALFIER ·
· Helen M. ASTERIS · Shawn AVENINGO-SANDERS ·
· Linda BARRETT · Duncan BERCE · Henry BLADON ·
· Howard BROWN · Michael H. BROWNSTEIN ·
· Rachel BURNS · Chuka Susan CHESNEY ·
· Jan CHRONISTER · Dave CLARK · Bethany CODY ·
· Beverly M. COLLINS · Linda M. CRATE · Tony DALY ·
· Mary DAURIO · Steve EVANS · Sarah GRAHAM ·
· Karen GROVE · Michael HALL · Mark HEATHCOTE ·
· Ryn HOLMES · Matthew HORSFALL ·
· Mark HUDSON · Valerie HUNTER ·
· Doug JACQUIER · Tim JARVIS ·
· Fiona M. JONES · Tarla KRAMER · Christine LAW ·
· Cynthia LESLIE-BOLE · Jan McCARTHY ·
· Rob McKINNON · Karla Linn MERRIFIELD ·
· John MOODY · Frank Wayne MOTTL ·
· Colleen MOYNE · Remngton MURPHY ·
· Claire NIEASS · Piet NIEUWLAND ·
· Carl 'Papa' PALMER · Gary PERCESEPE ·
· Alex ROBERTSON · Ruth Sabath ROSENTHAL ·
· Ed RUZICKA · Mir-Yashar SEYEDBAGHERI ·
· Martin SHAW · Chris STEWART · Carole THORPE ·
· Lydia TRETHEWEY · Lucy TYRRELL ·
· Lois Perch VILLEMAIRE · Maria VOUIS ·
· Lauren Bronwyn WAGNER · Alan WALOWITZ ·
· Allan J. WILLS · Emma WILSON · Melissa WONG ·

A Toast to the Tangerine

Cynthia Leslie-Bole

bless your compact components
nestled tight together
within a pungent peel

bless your juicy crescents
bound into orange moons
by pithy threads

bless your squat packages
of sunshine-turned-citrus
sweetening in community

bless your orbs of sustenance
suspended on our family tree
like contiguous circles of caring

bless your roots
that reach for what nourishes
and blindly feel their way forward
even in the dark of dirt
to spread a filagreed foundation
that holds you upright
while you grope toward god

bless your trunk
that shows spine
and the shine of your green leaves
that shelter others
and your bitter seeds carrying
holograms of wholeness
like the spirals twisting in our cells

bless you, ambassador
of the animate world
for showing us how to
be fully fruitful

Salt is the Taste of Christmas Holidays

Dave Clark

The sweat accumulated on thousand
Kilometre drives, racing summer's light.
The smack on my lips after a beach swim.
Newspaper-wrapped dinners of fish and chips.

Salt is the taste of Christmas holidays.

Rubbed into the reopened family wounds,
Debates and aches preserved for yearly bouts.
Eyes running as reminiscing unfolds
And as I sit with Dad at his graveside.

Salt is the taste of Christmas holidays.

Leftover ham watching Boxing's first ball.
Handfuls of popcorn munched with stars on screen.
Perspiration among bargain hunters.
Replenish after days baked by sun's glow.

Salt is the taste of Christmas holidays.

The Glow

Allan J. Wills

I give my lover
Three oranges
Juggling, juggling
Laughing, laughing
"I'll make you unhappy!"
My lover promises

I give my lover
A diamond ring
Pinfire sparkling
Flashing, Flashing
"I'm a destroyer!"
My lover promises

I give my lover
Two children
Vivacious and bright
Happy, happy
"Tell me no lies!"
My lover demands

Old and fat-bellied,
I ask my lover
"What more can I give you?"

"Lover, lover,
Fifteen years
Grey hair!
Another ten
Lit by the TV glow!"

Orange Glow

Remngton Murphy

We were kissing,
When all of a sudden

She disengaged her lips and said,
"It's a Marshmallow World."

Thereupon, I ejaculated—
Which is to say

Strictly in the verbal sense—
"What?!"

"Sure," she said. "That Dean Martin song,
Haven't you ever noticed

That like totally inaccurate lyric,
And the sun is red like a pumpkin head?"

"No," I replied. "Silly me,
I've never noticed it."

"Pumpkins aren't red," she explained.
And then, brushing back a permanent curl

And giving me this come-hither pout,
She said, "Whenever I sing that song

I always substitute another word:
For example, And the sun is red

Like a rigid head."
She bit her lip, and staring like a red-tailed hawk

Sizing up its prey,
She asked, "Don't you?"

Somehow at a loss for words,
I nevertheless managed

To blurt out, "Uh?"
"Whenever I think of bulging gourds,"

She went on, "I always visualize
This like Halloween jack-o-lantern

Grinning on my front door porch,
Suffused in this kind of orange sherbet

Woo-woo otherworldly glow."
And then, running a finger down my chest,

She made this kind of circle with her lips—
And as for telling you what happened next,

Well, suffice it to say—uh—
I better quit while I'm ahead.

Come and get it?

Mark Heatchote

'Come and get it?' What a happy phrase
it reminds me of The Waltons
... weren't they all gifted on the stage.
That family who lived in rural Virginia
in the Great Depression, lived hand to mouth;
Each like some poet master or sage
or a half-starved hermit-mouse about the house.
'Come and get it?' Jumping off the porch-swing,
'Come and get it?' Running down some mountain stream,
waving a dying torch glowing in the dark starlit gleam.
'Come and get it?' A ringing bell that sent
their hearts, ours ringing to and throw.
'Come and get it?' A candlelit table's glow;
wet feet shaking off the dirt and snow.
'Come and get it?' What happened to all that family time?
I guess it went out of fashion like poetry and rhyme.
'Come and get it?' They slavered around the mouth,
each one happy to live either North or South,
but today East or West, there is no place best.
Little did they know back then?
'Come and get it?' ... They were all blest.

Opal Becomes a Woman

Tobi Alfier

Her name was Opal—after her fiery eyes,
and the fire she lit in many a man's bones.

In earlier times she wore her shirt tight as sin
and a scowl just as sinful,

but there was a many-years-ago reason for that scowl,
that *keep away come hither* look at the same time,

and these days a reason for exactly the opposite—
the many necklaces wound around her neck,

fiery red, and orange hues of Mexican Opal,
each one a separate gift, not a devil among

the givers. Stones reflecting upward like light
brilliant with sunrise. Like the fields—

vibrant poppies with the same orange and honey hues.
Riding bareback and glowing on daddy's big ranch,

Opal talks softly to the horse, hums
a lullaby remembered from the old days.

Straight black hair blankets her like her horse's black mane,
silence hovers over the wider quiet of the colorful meadows.

Milonga Night

Jan McCarthy

My beams hug his tail lights
Window rolls cat-purr down
The night is jessamine,
  mock orange, heliotrope
I have turned to his sun
Feet in driving thongs throb,
High heels discarded,
Five hours of glued together
  sweaty dance
His eye-fire hooked me like Bathurst burrs
The house looms, smaller than expected,
He lights candles, smiles
And in the kitchen
Bare feet on night-cool stone,
I watch him, tiger-elegant,
the dip of shoulder that first drew me in,
  hear the clink of ice,
  watch coconut liqueur ooze,
  cushion of meltwater gather,
  the wind of grenadine through condensation

He pulps the fruit, pumping pips to swim
  like tadpoles, like something else
The tang of it, tarted with orange juice
He stirs and so do I,
  moving to join him
We could be dancing now
But we slowly sip, eyes flicking,
  all anticipation,
  delaying the delicious moment of
    our passion fruit cock tales

Over Easy

Michael H. Brownstein

This morning I entered
a world of orange rust,
no dreams of the living,
no keepsakes of the dead—
into the graying of snow.

You think this a poem of depression,
a storm of mold and disinterest—
but a songbird sings from her nest,
a cardinal flashes red.

Some mornings the world is a piss storm,
without sound and then a squirrel
runs one branch to another full of glee.

Search for the Prime Meridian
Greenwich July 2019

John Moody

Hot today,
as I contemplate smooth viridian
grass, parched straw yellow in patches
below the Royal Observatory.
Flawless blue, London's meridian sky.

A Thames skyline like an elegant 3-D
puzzle in shades of blue-green glass
and metal. A skyscraped business skyline.
Thames soup grey-green waters below;
thick-turgid slow wandering flow through fading
Empire's city. Windy hot air blasting.

Brisk sweaty walk to a meridian hill
in the days heat
I took this trip to Imperial history
claustrophobic
enough to celebrate a nation.

On my Greenwich right as I'm
Striding an incline from the river is
bygone beached Cutty Sark
encased in a glass blister, to be sure it stays

away from its days carrying Aussie wool and Clipper tea
feeding Empire's prime she sits like a long predatory
jawed fish caught in a glazed limpet reflecting
on a lost chunk of Empire.

Then on up past spread classical
columned grandeur of
empire's gestation & birth through
resurgent monarchy
national interest & competition
with the French — now a maritime museum.

Then an Observatory in Royal fashion for shipowners
and drowning sailors. '… so as to find out the much desired
Longitude of Places for the perfecting of the art of Navigation.'

Caught in the past's web, this National Maritime Museum
reflects a Brexit-raddled kingdom's fading consequence
in the world today — all we've got left is a meridian.

Then up the hot hill to bleached light blue
telescoped dome, leached drier still by
the tourist lice, from all the world here to wonder
then straddle the Prime Meridian —
though its hundreds of feet off zero degree
longitude they think they're east and west all at once.

Magnificent view over Thames laced London, from
a chunk of early empire now dry as a ship's biscuit
and too polluted to observe the stars.

Once making the seas safe for trade and
commerce, calculating distance east
and west of this supposed point of zero.
The world comes
here to sweltering Greenwich
to see time and distance begin.
A world should measure itself from here.
Splitting the juicy globe in to tangy
orange-like segments of trade.

Here centuries of painstaking
collected astronomical data — to show
my country's place in the world.
Assiduous observations over centuries
for the honour of prime earth position.
Can I live on past glories flowing from this hot, airless
over peopled little hill?

Here I'll rest in tourist din.
Greenwich is where all Brexits begin.

Seaham Beach, late evening

Rachel Burns

I watch you and your brother play with your toy cars
metallic red and blue, you build roads and bridges
from the wet sand. People walk their dogs along the sea front.
As the sun begins to set, we pick up the buckets and spades
and head back to the car park, passing the martial arts club
training on the beach, a group of mixed ages; small children
and men exercising. Twenty press-ups on the shingle,
backs silhouetted by the sun, blood orange.

The Snowed-In People

Karla Linn Merrifield

One must have a mind of bomb cyclones
and polar vortices uncorked. Throw
another log into the woodstove's glow.
Notch up the furnace. Plug in

electric blankets and space heaters.
Pull a comforter over your head.
Cuddle up a little closer if you can
against wicked cold air sourced

from Siberia, angry and impulsive,
Sharks from the Atlantic wash up frozen.
Oranges shrivel beneath rinds of ice.
Homeless lose limbs to frostbite's gangrene.

Cow, Trout, and Teepee

Frank Wayne Mottl

It's a wanted cow,
escaped from some yard,
or other,
means of release from
the doldrums of being a cow—unknown.

Dumb thing.
Only a step in the right direction.
Mack helped me past the cow,
its green cud chewing, spewing all
over the place.

Trout was a different story.
Lithe, silver streaky smart,
smart enough to guide our way
through the wooded bush, the clearing,
until finally,
the teepee glowed.

Burning Love

Henry Bladon

Would it somehow rekindle our love
if I offered to set fire to my head
(like Hendrix did with his guitar)
so that you might warm yourself on the heat
and enjoy the hypnotic glow of the flames?

Would that satisfy your masterplan
(like some sadistic smiling overlord)
or would it merely leave me
with nothing more than a chargrilled memory
of our relationship and a worthless pile of ash?

Someone else's disaster

Tarla Kramer

We are woken by yelps at 3am
from the folks across the road –
they are not partying this time.

Their backyard has an orange glow
of a barbecue out of control.
Flames from the garage climb higher,
fanned by an eerie wind from nowhere
and singe the house next door.

My son is gaming.
There's a fire, I tell him.
It's bad.
He wakes the others.

Mum gets her camera and snaps
but I just can't.
I've assumed my default crisis position
and am down on all fours.

Someone more level-headed than me
has called the fire brigade
but they take forever.

Where are they,
I pray and rock and groan.
But the siren never sounds.

While pyjamed folk stand helpless,
another level-headed person
makes a video on their phone
which we see on the news 15 hours later.

Suddenly they're here
six silent fire trucks.
Good thing too as the house is burning up –
we hear things going pop –
and ours might be next.

A man in all his gear
sends us inside – and shut the windows;
it's going to get smoky.
But Mum doesn't take any notice.
Not wanting to miss out, she's still outside.

The pyjama brigade ventures out again
when all is foam
and water runs down the street.
I bring Mum tea and
my daughters sit on the front lawn.

At last I make a video
for my youngest who wouldn't wake
so he can see the fire trucks.

Finally it's out.
The neighbours go back to bed
and try to sleep
except the ones with no home.

One crew stays,
lights blinking on til Boxing Day dawns.
Strobe like, they don't let us sleep.

In the morning while new crews
interview the family outside the ruin,
I take them Christmas goodies
and meet them after 30 years.

Then, praying they don't see
I sneak boogie boards into the car
because we're off to the beach.

Light Leaks In

Bethany Cody

Otherworldly auburn aura around
Your Cheezel-dusted fingertips.
I forgot to put on my glasses.
My hand on your chest
Makes a thousand passes.
Lounging in the afterglow,
Contented kisses from your lips.
Our faces illuminated by the
Fuzzy gloom of the TV screen,
We're scrolling through a thousand stories,
Some we've already seen.
Sweaty heat underneath these covers,
I'm up behind you,
We're holding each other,
Breathing in the scent of your
Scalp and fabric softener.
My retinas are dying so
It's mostly unsurprising
When irregular milky semicircles
Leap and flash and shimmer
Across the screen –
Additional special effects
From an unfit, defective gene.

The Moon Wears Winter's Veil

Mir-Yashar Seyedbagheri

the moon wears a whiter veil,
than she did a month ago
when autumn was young and the leaves danced
donning orange and gold in autumn's ballet
and I walked with strides and danced with the leaves
now she watches from slate blue shadows
luminous in nascent snow.
air thawed like war
I walk a little slower

how she can accept all this,
nights when charcoal-colored clouds envelop her
and darken the roads and valleys
like a critic clamoring for grim sensation
how can she glow when she emerges?
yet still she dons her white veils, although a little whiter
without complaint, she watches me
slouching along snow-covered country roads
she whispers her love

while I walk home, eyes hollowed

autumn smile dissolved in mud and ice

above ground

Carole Thorpe

cast out of a circus
without a future
an acrobat descends
over a city
from an orange and green
helicopter: she grips
a rope at sunrise
before rush hour
listens to birds trees

they open beaks and
                    boughs
a maple tree offers
        an olive branch
with one bird
singing a sonnet

above ground the acrobat
soft lands on the
                    olive branch
this city waking
looks skyward at a
        solar-powered
helicopter

She (who brought oranges to the sea)

Doug Jacquier

Silent-Time,
returning insistently
on anniversaries
of light and dark.
Mirror-Time,
encouraging reflection,
but lacking depth
in the sum of its parts.
Shadow-Time,
for those with their backs to the Sun
or those looking over their shoulder
to see where they've been.
History-Time,
which speaks for itself
in the language of the actors
and the victors.

I could tell you of a time
when She brought oranges to the sea
but you would only see its shadow in your mirror
and be silent
in the presence of an uncommon history.

Marie Curie Discovers Radium

Valerie Hunter

The cartoon makes it
amusing and innocuous,
Marie Curie faintly glowing
like some immortal goddess
or alien being,
set apart, a living pedestal
of light.

She teaches us
the value of science,
of perseverance,
of questioning the unknown,
all worthy lessons,
while also whispering
that monumental
discoveries are worth
our lives.

At the end of the cartoon,
she simply fades away,
with no mention made
of the lingering death
and the lead-lined coffin.

Paper Storm

Sara Abend-Sims

The day hasn't been terrible
not really not at all
I know this sounds far-fetched...
the lines of the bald man go on and on

terrible, I think and
try to stop his chatter
ending up with tears
with a smile on my face

the bleeding is important
the producer fairy-godmother says
she is frantic bossy, holding tissues
a soft bundle to smooth sweaty palms
to sooth our glowing foreheads

she wipes smiles off each face
specks of thin paper flutter in the air
land on her hair and cover my lap
dotting stars on the bald shining head

fairy dust and paper flakes
block our noses making voices hoarse
part of the production
our godmother yells
drowning lines and grumbles

turbulence swallowing our script
terrible   really,   really   terrible
paper specks dust bleeding
sweaty palms
a day in a life.

Bottom of My Heart

Lois Perch Villemaire

The bottom of my heart is crowded.
It's where condolences wait to be shared.
Where love for my family resides.
Where I feel emptiness for
Special ones lost,
Who will never be forgotten
or replaced.
Where there are empty spaces
That ache
Where regrets weigh heavy
Even though I forgive myself.
Where optimistic faith nests
When the world is in turmoil.
Continuing to believe
Words I heard as a child,
"Everything will be all right."
Where memories glow,
Preserving my parents
Forever, reflecting the best of times.
Where feelings are buried,
Bubbling up when least expected.
Where I find the inspiration to write,
Excavating to the very bottom,
Searching the deepest cavern,
Making certain it can expand.

Orange Tungsten Glow

Emma Wilson

Dank midnight percussive sesh, below the orange glow of the tungsten filament.

Deep in the echoes of pre-conspiracies we release the green drake and set it free to wind its smokey haze up to the eaves while we sway to the beat, a cool and easy feat of duplicitous tapping and rapping accompanying the sounds of Luna and Sol as they process through our ears and into our brains unable to contain breaking out of the frame of expectations a conflagration of musical notation creating soular elation under this

Orange.

Tungsten.

Glow.

Coral

Sarah Graham

We've been practising fluorescence
for so many years –
we're good at it now!
Come forward, admire
and don't be shy.
A little closer,
you're still out of reach.

The night-time is here, we want
to shine, and show off
our beautiful shapes –
so we glow.
Our tendrils wave gently
and we look benign,
but beware!

We can sting you if you come near.
Our arms will welcome you
but you won't escape.

Intelligent Orange Woman Seeks Lovely Man

Karen Grove

These words began my profile
on the Yahoo Personals site
orange being the colour of the fruit
that gives the colour its name
the colour of fire
the colour of my hair
the colour of my shirt in my photo
my most flattering colour

The man who would become
my second husband
thought orange might refer
to the Orange Order
his Irish Catholic father spoke of
the bigots who marched on July 12th
to celebrate William of Orange
and the Battle of the Boyne

He took a chance
and met me for coffee anyway
Sixteen years later
I am still an intelligent orange woman and
Lovely Man is still lovely

Laze

Lucy Tyrrell

Footage of volcanic activity,
breaking news from the Big Island,
geologists explain *laze*—
haze from churning orange lava
plunging into the Pacific.
It hisses, releases chemical fog-fumes,
drifts as particles that could burn lungs.

After dark, last hours
of a trip to Hawaii,
pull off the road,
grip binoculars,
view from afar
the molten fire of Kilauea.

A glimpse, no more
than an orange
ribbon, a burning
torch, but you could imagine
an entire lava landscape,
emergent power from fiery depths,
insouciant to roads and signs,
any infrastructure in its way.
Tumble-flow gushes,
oozing advances,
liquid-glow runways
birth more island,
flow to the sea.

Her Candle

Carl 'Papa' Palmer

So many candles I've never burned.
A marriage candle,
two first communion candles from my kids,
a bicentennial candle,
millennium candle.
So many candles I've never burned.

Her candle I've burned for over twenty years,
not every day, but most every day.
A memory of what once was,
of what we had
me and her,
her candle.
Originally voluptuously large,
beautifully ornate,
burning bright hot and fast.
We were young then.

Gradually her candle grew old,
became hollow.
Most of the outside still holding fast,
dusty with age,
the wick long lost,
in darkness temporarily filled
with a tea light candle.

Certain songs, movies or moods
seem to rekindle the freshness,
remind me of when her candle was new.

In the light of day reality blazes,
her candle actually an empty shell.
So hard to visualize as it once was,
as in last night's memory.

Beginning to wonder,
continuing to wonder,
if, after all this time,
I shouldn't just throw it out.
This foolish vigil,
this senseless old man,
end this memorial,
this ritual and move on.

But, as the room grows dark,
the many candles I've never burned
remain so.
A new tea light candle
and she is back.
We, me and her,
her candle
and my thoughts
of twenty years ago.

Her Prized Zinnias

Ruth Sabath Rosenthal

autumnal hues with bee-magnet centers.
In the planting, pearls of satisfaction
beaded Mother's cheeks — made her glow
head to toe. Each summer, till first frost,
zinnias fringed the pathway leading to
our side-door by the kitchen.

Mother loved her zinnias — their colors,
rich contrast to the dusty-rose brocade sofa
and light aqua cut-velvet of Father's chair,
each encased in a clear-plastic slipcover
that, in summer, made the backs of our thighs
stick to our seats and, in winter, felt

so unwelcoming. Not to mention, when
our new dining set arrived, Mother, keen
on keeping it pristine, moved *Lucky*,
my beloved canary, to the kitchen
to roost inches from the stove,
the nearby window rarely open;

and child that I was, I didn't protest
on my bird's behalf. Weeks later,
just home from school, I learned
Lucky had died, his cage given away.
Mother claimed she'd buried him
herself — didn't feel she could wait

till I got home. To this day I'm not
at all certain she actually buried *Lucky*
in the tiny backyard earthen patch
she'd pointed out — a mere blip
in the earth, a couple of feet from
her prized orange Zinnias.

This Poem is Brought to You by the Letter O

Shawn Aveningo-Sanders

Overindulgence
Overspending
Overeating
Overweight
Obesity
Oprah's
O Magazine.
Over-Achievers
Octomoms
Overtime and
Overworked at
Overstock.com
Oh No!
Overnight
Orange
Oompa Loompa
Occupies
Oval Office
Orating
Ostentatious
Obscenities

Over-the-net
OMG
Overwhelmed, I'm
Outta here.
Oh my God
Oh my God
Oh my God. At least there's still
One good thing left: the big
O
       —yeah, you know what I mean

Summer Evening Sunset

Linda Barrett

It comes once again
at six in the evening
the sun begins its descent
into the east.
An orange glowing sun
rests itself between
two gnarled oaks
standing sentry between
the left and right of
Route 611 in Warrington, Pa.
In my house,
under the picture window,
Gilded Queenie
gives off a burnished
Golden Retriever glow
as she sits with her head
raised, pondering
on the living room couch.

The Glow Inside

Lauren Bronwyn Wagner

I loved fearlessly
And he was strong
Like black coffee with a dash of whiskey
But beneath that he was soft

If you could see inside

He was rough
Like loose gravel roads
Like the back roads that lead to home
But he was quiet in his mind

If you could see inside

He danced with the darkness
That chased daylight away
Before the moon could rise
But his glow within was bright

If you could see inside

He was a gracious liar
Like the calm before the storm
A silken web of lies
But truth was all he left behind

If you could have seen inside

The House Defence

Rob McKinnon

Darkly ominous smoke clouds
had developed for hours,
radio reported a furious terror
progressing murderously closely.

Too late for a change of minds
pulses raced as fear began to pound,
studious plans had been developed
which needed precise implementation.

The pumps were started
dowsing began of equipment, vehicles
and all vegetation close to the house,
gutters were filled in intense anticipation.

Skies darkened as the manic flames came into view
heralded by sweeping evil embers
searching for fertile footholds
to initiate new terror.

Landing sinful cinders were soaked as best as possible
but their homicidal number increased
as the flames flashed uninhibitedly,
structures and trees infested joined the glowing corruption.

Radiant heat was the recognised dreaded assassin,
as the blazes advanced a calculated retreat was initiated
inside the house to the designated safe area.
Embers rained on the windows with macabre merriment.

As winds changed the capricious ferocity
altered its annihilating direction
and followed some other obliteration elsewhere.
Alleviating liberation for the hiding.

When safe to leave the house,
lingering spot fires were extinguished
and relief whelmed with realisation
that they had survived.

Tank Buster

Martin Shaw

It's sunny
motorbike's out
name changes for seasonal riders
Chris Spedding or
The Ton-Up-kid

cameras look dazed in the haze
they enforce slower highways
even the canals are faster
The One-Ounce-Kid!

police clampdown
as rubber gathers hot bitumen
like black snow

the new law
a fifty-metre riding distance
coronavirus?

visor down
I'm stopping my slobber
hitting the bobber
behind me
Harley Davidson shite
the riders open helmet
face-off

chrome looks pitted
as fly guts harden
Full Metal Jacket

a pig in the sky?
an air balloon?
Pink Floyd?
new album?
the distraction
perilous

it's not road-rage
but the 'road rages'
on pillion skin
like grating cheese

pop-pop
through the town.
posters of Costello
his lisp
the only talent left
charm the snake out

rubber washers
perishing
as a new cough mixture
of demon petrol
makes pipes hoarse
and sparkplugs glow

goofy kids,
give a thumbs-up
pensioners
give a thumbs down
no change there then

Alien Hunger

Tony Daly

Staring through a plasma shield shimmering with eerie glow,
lending effervescent luminosity to swirling landscape's flow.
Everything seems foreign though I've known it since my birth.
It's been four generations since my ancestors left the earth.
Don't know what it's worth but this place never felt like home,
so I sit and daydream of all the solar systems I'll roam.
Once I leave this sheltered dome on a ship that I've concealed,
I will search for a planet with a golden wheaten field.
Imagine what it will yield – crisp and fresh from soil food
of which the ancient legends tell, not tasteless and crude
like this synthesized mush exudes. I've only known alien hell.
So I'll follow this compelling dream to shed this plasma shell.

Fire Tending

Ed Ahern

They are rare individuals.
I know them immediately,
their hearth fire radiance
draws me to their warmth,
thrown off without demands
for attention or favor.
I bask in the unmeasured glow
of their selfless self-focus,
rest in the calmness
of their frictionless inner unity.
I am not envious
of their flickering shimmer,
their inner heat of coals
and let them gently radiate,
not advice or instruction,
but healing perspective.

when fruit is in the seed there is no orange

Chris Stewart

before orange people begin
to peel their skin they sleep
in layers of albedo

it takes juice to carve
windows in pumpkin shells
to scoop eye-shaped seeds

out of orange bodies when
you can't tell where stones
end and flesh begins

when people are not
quite gold I perceive
them colourless but

what do I know about
orange people? the truth
is the more flame I lick

the more citrus I sniff
the more rust I scratch
the more pennies I hear

the colours I see in
orange are my business

Cypress

Ed Ruzicka

Slack, inky upstream, the creek
gurgles, shoots silvered over roots
where four cypress vault in sheer,
vertical assent. Trunk's muscles lift
in columns, stiff as cock's surge.

On tree bark a tender moss or fungus,
almost talcum, has formed. Beaded
as rust, but softer, this growth

is the tangerine sun shows when it rolls
out of the east to glaze wave crests,
suffuse mists, throw shimmers
of tangerine into shore trees.

As sun lifts from the tabernacle of the sea
earth itself forgets what dream
we have all been drowned in together.

That talcum, that fungus is softly mottled
as rust on metal where it forms a broad
band around the bases of these four cypress.
I begin to think that dawn is there,
still glows tangerine, where these cypress
once began to set their rings into daylight.
Still there at the site of their early sprouting
while they lift themselves into sun,
put their faces into starlight each night.

Birds flit in, nest, squabble. Small creatures
make a home, insects, lichens, mosses.
I, who am always forgetting, have forgotten
to tell you how every muscle inside me
aches toward the sun every day and I remember
too little of my childhood and do not understand
the great thrusts that formed me, but still
I rise and go into the heat of day. I put
my face into starlight every night.

Goldfish

Tim Jarvis

I remember when I was eight
All I wanted was a puppy
I got a goldfish
But when you have nothing, you can't be picky
It didn't do tricks
It didn't like to be petted
It didn't do anything really
Just stared at the wall with glassy eyes
Hell, it wasn't even gold
It was orange
Orange
One of the only words in the English language nothing rhymes with
What a useless piece of shit of a pet
And yet here I am
A dozen or so bad decisions and I turned into one
Me, a goldfish
It's not just the orange colour of my clothes
Or the wide eyes of my dread
It's because I'm worthless
Small

My life is used to teach children about death
Taken from my natural home
And forced into this alien world
Surrounded by the cold walls of my container
Which I pace around and around endlessly
Like toothpaste circling the sink
Sometimes the guards tap on the sides for amusement
Sometimes they bring me bits of food
Damn, at least that goldfish had a castle
If only I was that little sucker
So, I could forget about my days, every day
And live in ignorance that tomorrow I'll get flushed

when the sun feels too heavy

Linda M. Crate

the day begins as it ends
with a carnelian glow
of sunset
lashed with other vibrant hues
until night kisses day to sleep,
and i feel as if i carry all of my weight
in the day until sleep comes
to take me to my dreams;
and the moon becomes my rescuer
i suppose that it makes sense
mothers always protect their children—
she reminds me sometimes
to be calm,
other times she reminds me i was
born to make waves;
she always reassures me that i am beautifully
even when i don't fully shine
out in the darkness—
and she is the sweet song that breaks me
of my chains
when the sun feels too heavy on my shoulders.

Tears of sky

Piet Nieuwland

On an evening of withering rain and forgetful moisture /
       Cardinal spaces, torrents and lava
We listen to abandoned voices of ruins / in the anthropogenic strata
Overlooking a hungry ocean /
       Night collapses onto the edge of an uncertain dawn
The wind breaks into a thousand pieces
Your liquid eyes are carried on silent wings /
Beneath the silk of perfect meaning
      Have you got blue eyes /
        Have you got grey eyes /
          Have you got brown eyes /
Weeping tears through an hour glass of orange roses

that colour

Matthew Horsfall

No words to catch the colours,
the threatening plumes iridescent,
so frozen in time we stood
choking under morning dusk.
What could we cram in the back of the car
in less than a minute? The weirdest colours
you could never imagine,
the strange colours defying description:
blackish orange, pinkish green, a glowing horizon.
We *were* the news, we were faster than websites
in meltdown, pages not refreshing, apps freezing.
The sky fell and we took bad advice
clarity and confusion merged into one.

No time for poetics, no paint could capture
the gorgeous powdered clouds,
the gentle rain of burning leaves,
ashy snowflakes falling, forbidden hues, melting streets.
It was no time for words, it can't be real it was real.
I knew it could happen, I never thought it would happen.
We were only home for three days before the same wind blew again,
the same evil rainbow. It chased us into the ocean
past the low tide mark, waves of smoke against north-east currents.
I blinked and felt soot in my eyes, there was nowhere we could hide,
it never seemed real the sight of those closing curtains.
I thought to myself this is how it ends –
trying to describe *that* colour.

Portal

Howard Brown

To the east, the glow of a full moon filters
through the towering pines, an
ethereal presence in the darkness of night.

For a breathless moment that shining orb
vanishes behind a bank of drifting clouds,
then reappears and I begin to think of it
differently, metaphorically, if you will.

Not as what we know the moon to be,
but as a portal through which we get a
glimpse of an endless ocean of light
which might lie just beyond the reach
of our ordinary senses.

Seven days later, that same moon has
now been reduced to a pale, orange
crescent. And somewhere in the distance,
an owl is calling: *do not dither, friend,* I
hear it say, *do not dither, for the portal is
fast closing!*

Sonnet for Serrano

Lydia Trethewey

immersion in a resonant space
the saviour, crucifix bright
in the hymn-deep vessel
synchronous vibration monistic
body dissolves into glowing light
into golden paradise vault

a scandal evolves, the work vandalized
glass hammer-cracked with righteous
malice, an exalted body in sacrifice
a small plastic cross, defiled
artwork reviled as blasphemy and
hateful abjection, crass, they say

(the figure of the lord submerged
in a jar of the artist's piss)

Enlightenment

Colleen Moyne

We had never heard of persimmons
until we bought the house in Salisbury.

There, outside the back door
was a leafy, green tree
adorned with curious globes,
all sweet and plump and golden.

'Got me beat,' my husband remarked,
as he walked around it, scratching his chin.
That year we let the birds have their fill,
scooping the remains into the bin.

'They're persimmons,'
a friend observed one day –
the day of our enlightenment.

And so, year two – somewhat selfishly –
we netted the tree
and kept the birds away.

I was pregnant then,
and suddenly that leafy green tree
adorned with curious globes,
all sweet and plump and golden

became my obsession
and my addiction.

Every morning I would walk around it,
looking for the ripe,
desperate to have my fill.
I remember still the rumbling tummy regrets
– an unwelcome side-effect.

But the trade-off of the smooth flesh
and honey-sweet juice
could not keep me away.
I ate them every day.

Perhaps that's why
my baby girl was born
all sweet and plump and golden.

For Hannah

Jan Chronister

Because you were born
this morning, I felt
the glow of life in the aftermath
of an early storm. My stomach
stopped hurting, my head quit
aching, my fears of your birth
blew away like smoke at dawn.
Because tonight at the end
of your first day on earth
the sky flamed behind
Spirit Mountain, I knew
it was good. Your life
is a blessing. Welcome.

Oranges and Plums

Ryn Holmes

Round
fragrant
succulence is shyly concealed
high in leafed branches of summer's shade.
Bright titian and deep burgundy
drip sun-warmed nectar,
waiting for her – the barefoot child
lazily curled into a notch
between two branches,
reading.

Why did you burn

Chuka Susan Chesney

Why did you burn

your brand new lamb
Grandpa bought you for Easter
while I was on the phone

with my bible study friend
about the crullers we'll provide
for our ladies' Jubilee
this eventide

I was standing by the counter
next to the bowl of figs
considering which congregant
I should have called next

when I saw you sashay
to the stove with your Lamby
You stuck her on the burner
turned up the heat

Next thing I noticed
was a turquoise flambeau
then a glow of harvest gold
consumed her acrylic curls

I screamed
turned off the flame
You wore your chiffon slip

Got the scarlet flyswatter
and I began to hit
your bare-skinned thighs
your arms your head

You shouted Mommy
stop today we learned in Sunday
School about incinerating lambs
to placate God

The Glowing Sticks

Mark Hudson

Back in the seventies, everybody smoked,
and as a kid, I was curious. My mother was a
smoker, so I would just steal a cigarette from
her pack, and go in my room and smoke it,
and the house always smelled like smoke, so
I never got caught.

One night in third grade, my friend
Allen slept over, a fellow smoker, and we
both had cigarettes. We were smoking
in my room, when the rug caught on fire.
We put it out, but there were black marks
where the orange glow of the cigarette
fire burned the rug. I told my parents,
"We were playing with matches, and
the rug caught on fire."

So my parents made me write an
essay on why it's bad to play with matches.
They were never good at meting out punishment.

Nonetheless, because of that, I quit
smoking. I didn't pick it up again till the
mid-eighties, when I started smoking
again and getting drunk with friends.

One night, walking by New Trier
high school in Winnetka, a rich suburb,
I had been drinking with friends and
lit up a cigarette. I must've taken a
deep drag, because there was a long,
orange glowing cherry dangling off
the cigarette. I said to my friends,
"Look, it's a dagger…Mick Jagger!"
My friend Chris laughed and said,
"Hudson, you're the best!"

Years later, when I had a two
and a half pack a day habit, my
next door neighbor encouraged me
to quit. I went to a stop smoking clinic,
and a man named Joel Spitzer saved
my life. My grandfather, a smoker
who I never met, died of lung cancer.
My mom died of cancer, not related to smoking.
Today, I honor them by never using glowsticks.

Naturofen

Duncan Berce

A droplet nestles in between
The ridges of a blade of green,
Sparkling with a single ray,
The first of all to come today.

Upon this tiniest of bites
Shimmer fractalizing sights,
Life reflected upside down,
Bend to smile from the frown

Gentle is the meadow breeze,
Dancing are the willow trees.
Were I a feather, long I'd fly
Upon the current of a sigh.

Leave your shoes and socks behind
For your older self to find.
Drink the grass between your toes,
Breathe the earth in through your nose.

Churning butter underground,
Everything here can be found.
Bones and blood and faeces crawl
Into what becomes us all.

Pants and shirts, they too can go,
Naked, you are sure to know,
Though, not the kind you think you might,
An earthen texture hugging tight.

Stripped to bare, just watch and feel
A soothing ointment to the ill.
Close your eyes and hear the bees
Buzz beneath the swaying trees.

Falling distant ocean rain
Calls a yearning, silent pain,
Dragging at the fog and cloud
Amidst which, clarity is found.

Draining free and draining fast,
Static wobbles to the past,
Silencing the arteries,
Still as ever aging leaves.

Death of ego, death of thought
Dying oughtn't, dying ought.
Keep it simple, watch the sheep,
Ever have they restful sleep.

Hear no voice, no distant song,
Whooshing car or bustling throng,
Sense the clouds above so high
Slowly peel thought from your mind.

Time alone in nature heals
Pain from what a human feels.
Easy on the zephyr, know
Peace to match the springtime glow.

Winter's Kiss

Mary Daurio

The power flickers, down, dim
And is gone, taking away the light
Into darkness, we blindly swim
Thick and heavy this snowy night

Bring out the coal oil lamp so old
Around its orange-hued gentle glow
Many a tall tale has been told
To this gleaming shore, we go

Up above the moon shines bright
And every star sparkles pristine white
Nocturnal animals find hidden bliss
In this blustery, blessed, winter's kiss

That Hypnotic Glow

Helen M. Asteris

The future's bright, the future's orange,
And it was.
Bathed in bronze, warm with anticipation
We stood with beady eyes and innocent smiles
Grinned vacuously into the 3G,
And poked those we'd forgotten.

Bent and beaming into open claws
We welcomed the immediacy, the vapid here and now-ness,
Paddle in my online glow, see how fabulous I am!
Brazenly we declared previous privates public,
And marvelled at horizons unfolding,
While shoulders and souls shrank.

Then 4 dispatched 3, now it's all 5G,
02 became better than air.
And our providers, be they repeating vowels or verbs,
Made our plans, learned our lines and set our limits.
No longer hunter gatherers, instead,
Host arbiters of time and text.

And our lust watched as we turned to new toys.
Apples and androids learned to defile more than Eve.
Enticing ergonomic design with a wipe clean finish
Vibrating snugly where no human longer need go.
Dispatching pleasures of the flesh to the palm of your hand,
Gratifying that hedonism we've personally tailored for you.

And so dear beloved user, enjoy my digital sandstorm,
Swipe on through this churning, insentient stream,
Keep conducting your cloud of unreasonable bees.
Trying to make sense of this world on a 3 x 5 screen,
Keep downloading your dream, that hypnotic glow
will eventually suffocate your spirit,
And its quiet little scream.

Coalbrookdale

Michael Hall

The furnace belches bright
and all about the landscape rosy glows.
Darkness cowers, put to flight;
a new age dawns midst fire and smoke.
Horses heave and workers strain,
enslaved to feed the fiery beast
whose ever hungry maw demands.
Two peasants pause and gaze,
their presence signal to an idyll past.
And as a backdrop to this scene,
Selene etches silver clouds;
stark contrast to the ruddy Hell
that spits and hisses centre stage.

I marvel at the artist's skill to capture,
on a canvas scarcely three feet broad,
the incandescent heat of change,
the revolution taking shape
in this small place called Coalbrookdale.

The Devil's kitchen smokes no more.
The Bedlam foundry hammers silenced long ago,
replaced today by tourist clamour,
stentor guides and ringing tills.
The sky is clear in Ironbridge now,
the air is clean, the sunshine bright.
No coalsmoke clouds to blot out sun,
no sulphur scent or hint of grime.
But here's a thought to ponder as you view.
Would those two peasants captured,
standing on the hill, still pause and gaze,
amazed at what now sets this place alight?
Or would they now be manning tills
and serving meals and posing,
in their period cozzies, for endless selfies
begged by eager crowds who throng this site?

Summer

Claire Nieass

Summer sun warming my weary bones
and life rises up within me
Others complain about the heat
but not I, for I love summer

Long days packed full of activity
time outside with family and friends
children playing in the pool
cool water beckoning me to unwind

Such glorious feelings remind me
to make the most of this season
and yet all too soon
I am yearning for summer again

Sweet

Beverly M. Collins

The fields waved like a crowd of
party-goers in motion. Orange tops of
flowers danced everywhere the eye
could see.

The pour of rain was as good for them as
Grandma's meal was for us on most Sunday
evenings. Chatter circled the dinner table
under the watchful glow of 3 large candles
anchored in the table's center.

The chicken dinner burned that night. However,
gossipy events of our week streamed as topic
of conversation until the sharing exhausted
itself into the sip of coffee, peach cobbler
and a side game of checkers that was just right.

Who knew those moments could morph
into pure gold. Wrapped in all the warmth a
memory could unroll. So laughable and simple.

Rainbow Fish

Melissa Wong

Remember when we went on a date to the Aquarium?
It was my first time in that giant, expensive fishbowl
The soft flirtation in my voice echoed off glass fish tanks
See it in my eyes and maybe taste the words on my lips

I stared dumbly at schools of fish and starfish
We gazed at sea urchins sitting upon thrones of coral
While a Nemo swam by in a flash of luminous scales
Oh, you say that species of fish is called a clownfish

Oceans might divide us and time may drag us apart
But that will never stop us, not now, not ever
Hear me across the distances between us
I love you and I'll say it until you're sick of hearing it

But the greatest sunken treasure in this boat's the jellyfish
Jellyfish that change like leaves in the fall
They'd change colour from pink to orange before our eyes
I instantly wanted one as a pet but you said 'they'd sting you'

As you cover my small hand with your pretty fingers
I feel your warm skin and I know where I belong
I find my place and know love will hold us together
Next time, I'll buy whatever you want from the gift shop

Message from a Starfish
Fromia Polypora

Maria Vouis

The sea is choppy today,
I plunge into the water,
green seaweed waves me
a wild whiplash 'hello'.

The starfish seem sleepy
but they're secretly busy,
winglets up like planes landing
they sift flotsam soup for a feed.

Then, splat my eye catches
Fromia polypora:
the leggy supermodel
of the starfish world.

Fluoro traffic-light-orange,
her arms akimbo in welcome
but the colour of caution,
she semaphores me:
                    mixed messages.

Autumnal Twilight – South Australia

Alex Robertson

This corkscrew action
Of the Earth around the Sun
Expanding the universe
And allowing day and night
    as the globe spins
Around this yellow dwarf
Visible light for humans
Displaying fiery palates in Earth's sky
The mid-latitudes driving cold front patterns
Dependent on cloud and humidity
Resplendent sunsets in the Gulf areas
Westerly waters teasing pink and purple clouds
In the last hours of sunlit glow

Shepherds taking warning
With the red sky in morning
Russet landscapes in agricultural areas
Turning sods with iron rich clays
        for wine, sheep and grain
The Hills hide Autumnal colours in their valleys
Deciduous trees mark this Australian 'orange season'
Flooding the ground with leaf litter
Before the Polar maritime winter blasts
        travel from the Southern Ocean
Cooling the coastal Plains and Riverland
Found with fog and frost on shorter days

Further North
Clear skies and auburn scenes
Cattle grids and fattened cattle and fences
        the only mark of outback settlement
On wide horizons
Reflected by treeless flat topography
Apart from rare mountain ranges
Covered by saltbush and desert plants
Campfires leaching the Earth's colour
When freezing temperatures douse the ochred coals
Swags and sleeping bags
        providing warmth for slumbered humans
Ready for another day in southern Terra Australis

The Collected Letters of My Daughter

Alan Walowitz

No *Hi, Dad, w'sup?* but a texted *TTYL*.
This is the way she holds me off.
Never privy to her late-night whereabouts,
all I want is: When is she coming home?
Instead she writes *L8R*, by which she means
there'll be a blue moon in the black sky
before I find out. Then I make my plea:
Come on. Not fair. I gotta know.
but all I get is *STBY*, and indeed it sucks to be me,
but *WTF*, this is all I've got,
till I try *TMIRLAGOITES*,
because she used to be such a curious child—
and I do get a, *WDYM?* I write:
The moon is rising like a giant orange in the eastern sky—
thinking how we used to like to look at it together
as it faded to lemon the higher it got,
then eggshell white no larger than a child's thumb held
back and forth to her eye in the black and blue of the early night.

And she writes, *WKEWL, OM,*
which means she's not at all impressed, but I ask, *OM?*
because I'm desperate for any letters she can spare for me.
Old Man, she replies, full length, after making me wait,
and then, a moment later, *LMAO.*
I'm happy she's happy,
though it's a shame an ass might come so easily off
when I'd prefer hers intact, laughing,
and right here beside me.

Stripey Puss

Christine Law

The kitten with the white and orange
Zig-Zag markings looked up at them.
Purring,
"Oh, Mum," said Mary, "he's trying to talk."
Mildred smiled. "Lets think of a name.
There's Marmalade or Ziggy."

"Marmaduke sounds better."
"Agreed," said Mildred.
She didn't care about a name,
All she wanted was a cat to
Get rid of the vermin from
Next door's pigeons.

Forbidden Colour

Fiona M. Jones

This is the hue that the poets eschew,
the shade they will always evade.

They'll go downtown in gowns of brown,
and they're often seen sporting green.
White's all right but not at night;
they're happier, I think, in pastel pink.
Occasionally they hurtle, too reckless, into purple,
but they soon go back to cautious black,
or maybe red instead.

They'll willingly follow their fellows in yellow,
whether citrusy jello or willowy mellow.
Grey is a way to say
when they're feeling blue, but blue again will always do
for shirt for me and jeans for you
or suede-style dancing shoe.

And yet, for the record, it's different abroad.
Peut-etre qu'en France le poete il danse dans
tout un melange de vetements orange?

anywhere

Gary Percesepe

on any night you wish
look down your street

observe your empty room
an abandoned field
the elevator in city hall

no sudden passion
no surge of desire
no air disturbed

she will appear
like a cutting stone
her laughter a fresh sword

small nose framing her face
arms encircling your waist
her mouth of kisses

the glow of her teeth
will become the lights
of the city you left.

When I'm Jesus

Steve Evans

When I'm Jesus
the world glows weird.
Nails spring up from the ground,
the wind blows through
the holes in my hands,
I know the words of a thousand songs,
my suit is perfect
and I gleam like a newborn,
stepping out the door each morning,
the gun in my pocket a token
of my affection for the world.

He'll pick up the pieces, won't he?
He loves us all,
even you,
but me especially.

About Truth Serum Press

Established in 2014, Truth Serum Press is based in Adelaide, Australia, but publishes books from authors in all parts of the English-speaking world.

Like sister presses Pure Slush Books and Everytime Press, Truth Serum Press is part of the Bequem Publishing collective.

Truth Serum Press has published novels, novellas, and short story collections.

We also publish smaller, shorter poetry collections.

Sometimes, when the mood strikes us, we publish multi-author anthologies. Generally, we publish fiction … and sometimes (just sometimes) we publish non-fiction.

We publish in English, and we would gladly publish in other languages if we understood them.

We like books that take us to new places, to new experiences and inside new minds and hearts.

We also like to laugh.

Visit our website at https://truthserumpress.net/.

Also from TRUTH SERUM PRESS

truthserumpress.net/catalogue

- *Verdant* Truth Serum Vol. 5
  978-1-922427-04-5 (paperback) 978-1-922427-05-2 (eBook)
- *Indigomania* Truth Serum Vol. 4
  978-1-925536-03-4 (paperback) 978-1-925536-84-3 (eBook)

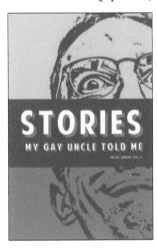 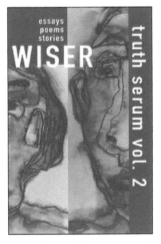

- *Stories My Gay Uncle Told Me* Truth Serum Vol. 3
  978-1-925536-86-7 (paperback) 978-1-925536-87-4 (eBook)
- *Wiser* Truth Serum Vol. 2
  978-1-925101-31-7 (paperback) 978-1-925101-32-4 (eBook)

Also from TRUTH SERUM PRESS

truthserumpress.net/catalogue

 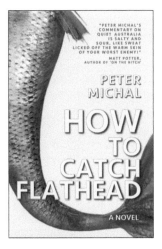

- *True* Truth Serum Vol. 1
  978-1-925101-29-4 (paperback) 978-1-925101-30-0 (eBook)
- *How to Catch Flathead* by Peter Michal
  978-1-925536-94-2 (paperback) 978-1-925536-95-9 (eBook)

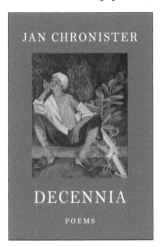 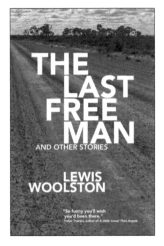

- *Decennia* by Jan Chronister
  978-1-925536-98-0 (paperback) 978-1-925536-99-7 (eBook)
- *The Last Free Man* by Lewis Woolston
  978-1-925536-88-1 (paperback) 978-1-925536-89-8 (eBook)

Also from TRUTH SERUM PRESS

truthserumpress.net/catalogue

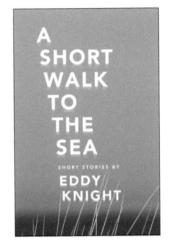

- *Filthy Sucre* by Nod Ghosh
  978-1-925536-92-8 (paperback) 978-1-925536-93-5 (eBook)
- *A Short Walk to the Sea* by Eddy Knight
  978-1-925536-01-1 (paperback) 978-1-925536-02-7 (eBook)

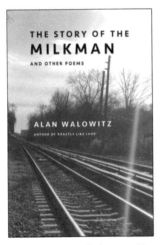

- *The Story of the Milkman* by Alan Walowitz
  978-1-925536-76-8 (paperback) 978-1-925536-77-5 (eBook)
- *Minotaur and Other Stories* by Salvatore Difalco
  978-1-925536-79-9 (paperback) 978-1-925536-80-5 (eBook)

Also from TRUTH SERUM PRESS

truthserumpress.net/catalogue

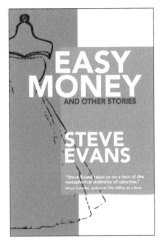 

- *Easy Money* by Steve Evans
  978-1-925536-81-2 (paperback) 978-1-925536-82-9 (eBook)
- *The Book of Acrostics* by John Lambremont, Sr.
  978-1-925536-52-2 (paperback) 978-1-925536-53-9 (eBook)

- *Square Pegs* by Rob Walker
  978-1-925536-62-1 (paperback) 978-1-925536-63-8 (eBook)
- *Cheat Sheets* by Edward O'Dwyer
  978-1-925536-60-7 (paperback) 978-1-925536-61-4 (eBook)

Also from TRUTH SERUM PRESS

truthserumpress.net/catalogue

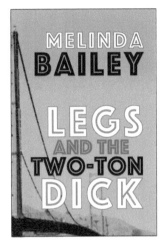

- *The Crazed Wind* by Nod Ghosh
  978-1-925536-58-4 (paperback) 978-1-925536-59-1 (eBook)
- *Legs and the Two-Ton Dick* by Melinda Bailey
  978-1-925536-37-9 (paperback) 978-1-925536-38-6 (eBook)

- *Dollhouse Masquerade* by Samuel E. Cole
  978-1-925536-43-0 (paperback) 978-1-925536-44-7 (eBook)
- *Kiss Kiss* by Paul Beckman
  978-1-925536-21-8 (paperback) 978-1-925536-22-5 (eBook)

Also from TRUTH SERUM PRESS

truthserumpress.net/catalogue

- *Inklings* by Irene Buckler
  978-1-925536-41-6 (paperback) 978-1-925536-42-3 (eBook)
- *On the Bitch* by Matt Potter
  978-1-925536-45-4 (paperback) 978-1-925536-46-1 (eBook)

- *Too Much of the Wrong Thing* by Claire Hopple
  978-1-925536-33-1 (paperback) 978-1-925536-34-8 (eBook)
- *Track Tales* by Mercedes Webb-Pullman
  978-1-925536-35-5 (paperback) 978-1-925536-36-2 (eBook)

Also from TRUTH SERUM PRESS

truthserumpress.net/catalogue

- *Luck and Other Truths* by Richard Mark Glover
  978-1-925101-77-5 (paperback) 978-1-925536-04-1 (eBook)
- *Hello Berlin!* by Jason S. Andrews
  978-1-925536-11-9 (paperback) 978-1-925536-12-6 (eBook)

 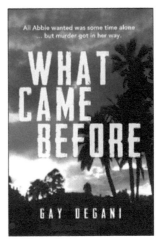

- *Deer Michigan* by Jack C. Buck
  978-1-925536-25-6 (paperback) 978-1-925536-26-3 (eBook)
- *What Came Before* by Gay Degani
  978-1-925536-05-8 (paperback) 978-1-925536-06-5 (eBook)

Also from TRUTH SERUM PRESS

truthserumpress.net/catalogue

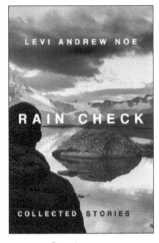 

- *Rain Check* by Levi Andrew Noe
  978-1-925536-09-6 (paperback) 978-1-925536-10-2 (eBook)
- *Based on True Stories* by Matt Potter
  978-1-925101-75-1 (paperback) 978-1-925101-76-8 (eBook)

 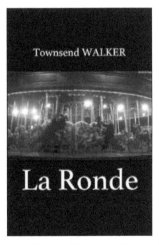

- *The Miracle of Small Things* by Guilie Castillo Oriard
  978-1-925101-73-7 (paperback) 978-1-925101-74-4 (eBook)
- *La Ronde* by Townsend Walker
  978-1-925101-64-5 (paperback) 978-1-925101-65-2 (eBook)

Travel books from EVERYTIME PRESS

https://everytimepress.com/everytime-press-catalogue/

 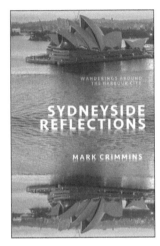

- *Perro Callejero* by Darren Howman
  978-1-925536-96-6 (paperback) 978-1-925536-97-3 (eBook)
- *Sydneyside Reflection* by Mark Crimmins
  978-1-925536-07-2 (paperback) 978-1-925536-08-9 (eBook)

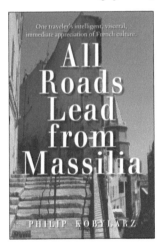 

- *All Roads Lead from Massilia* by Philip Kobylarz
  978-1-925536-27-0 (paperback) 978-1-925536-28-7 (eBook)
- *Lenin's Asylum* by A. A. Weiss
  978-1-925536-50-8 (paperback) 978-1-925536-51-5 (eBook)